THE HOLLOW VALE

T0345992

THE HOLLOW VALE

A POEM BY

JAMES TURNER

CAMBRIDGE

AT THE UNIVERSITY PRESS

1947

CAMBRIDGE
UNIVERSITY PRESS

University Printing House, Cambridge CB2 8BS, United Kingdom

Cambridge University Press is part of the University of Cambridge.

It furthers the University's mission by disseminating knowledge in the pursuit of education, learning and research at the highest international levels of excellence.

www.cambridge.org
Information on this title: www.cambridge.org/9781107487352

© Cambridge University Press 1947

First published 1947
First paperback edition 2015

A catalogue record for this publication is available from the British Library

ISBN 978-1-107-48735-2 Paperback

PROLOGUE

What I have been and shall be
Are two sides of a looking-glass,
Polished and unpolished, blurred and bright,
And, sometime, silver as for a bride
    Or a home-coming.

I shall take the long road home in the dark.
Yet no man knoweth his home,
Only the road thither and the ache
Which turns him over the hills,
Puts his hand to the smoke-green bole of the oak,
Lifts his eyes into the moonfed darkness.
The long road home in the dark!
And home, whether it be a place
Where feeds the raven, or a high hill
On which rises a temple built in white stone,
Or the hallucination of a spirit along a lane
Trodden and re-trodden always towards the light.

    If I shall raise my hands
    That the weight of my feet
    May be drawn from the earth,
    Then it is time to deny myself
    And, with curving, to destroy
    The shibboleths of youth,
    The ardent love of strangeness.

I will turn my feet now under the dark
Where I have felt an eternal pulse,
I will turn my feet homewards,
Forsake wandering over the plains
Of the spirit depressed,
And down beside the river
Where the osiers are golden rods
I will take, homewards, my shell of experience.
There was a way bright with petals
And polished buds; and there was a way
Golden with empty brass upon which my feet
Trod as in a burning wilderness,
And there was a way about me and about.
The soul fell down into the dark night,
        Into the abyss
Of serpents born of a hollow wish.
The serpent's eye with green light blazed,
The scorpion like a clot of blood,
The hooded cobra drummed out death.
Here the pit, its mouth steel-riveted
        Fired with a brazen dark.
The rising figures of life-myth
Tear at the mind and bite the memory,
Potent to claim the soul turned homeward,
And only at the throat a longing thirst
Like tiger's fangs in a green jungle.

Fiery liquid burn in me
With a fierce intensity,
Burn my eyes and burn my brain,
Burn my lips with fearful pain.

Fiery liquid burning bright,
Burn my taste and burn my sight,
Sear my flesh and sear my hair,
Consume with flame me everywhere.
That of the fire I be a part,
Burn, at last, within my heart.

THE QUEST

How brave the flesh on a setting-out,
The mind like a blade of Toledo
Swift and flashing. For the quest
Is nothing but a going-forth into the hollow vale,
Into the winds; and the leave-taking,
The last turn of the head towards the homestead,
The stirrup cup from hands of younger brother,
Is to the mind an adventure.
This is the sought-for cup with silver blazon,
The chalice and the grail,
End and beginning, hate and love,
The spectre of a shield; echo of cloth of gold.

Who goes forth to find what?
The hands shall be like empty stone
Of a statue, and the magic words
Shall avail no more than the laugh of a toad
Against the shut doors, the stone templates.
Flesh of my flesh shall the journey be,
And the bone shall appear beyond the flesh
With the heart torn out and held aloft,
And the apex of a head lifted
As the dome of a cathedral over the crowds
Passing in at the doors, or passing out.
Black shall the flesh be, burnt in the fire

Of the endless journey over desolate tracks
Where breath is turned into stone,
And the green bird chants to a lonely waste.

And the journey will hold magic.
But who shall say that is no trap
To have heard the song of the maiden over the shore,
Or to have hung beads on the moon
In the lazy days, when purpose waned,
          Journey forgotten?

Come now to the terrifying place
And behold the earth like waste of lead,
The leaden waterless desert, greying to dust,
Snaring the feet with its dusty weight,
All, all is gone save the bird of prey.
Others have spoken of the journey,
The lonely heath, desolation in places;
And coming home again have told
Their traveller's tales of squalid holes
Where serpent coils to spring,
Of battles with intangibilities,
The fierce grip of the winds in the wastes.
One has said of the mysterious place
That there is nothing there but God only,
And yet nothing strange. Everything

In that place was familiar,
Well known and nourished.

Who has listened to a traveller's tale
And did not wish to take his horse,
His spears and his dogs, then, at that moment,
Into the unknown? Brave is the flesh
Before the exaggerated story
And the hearth-worn adventure.
Or who would mark the scars on an old face,
Or stay to enquire whence they came?
For when the day is come surely the sun
Is token enough of possibility
And promise of success, that where one failed
Another will not fail?·

Who now will deny the green bird,
Now that the day is come
When brother's handshake is a welcome end
To dreaming and long wish-fulfilment?
Follow the bird down the hill
Into the hollow vale. Spread out the fine mantle
Over your shoulders till you come
Where pride is bitten in the dust,
And the asphodel melts into the desert.

Many have been and have their tokens;
Some returned not, but their end

Is the high end of all God's adventures,
A place for the lonely heart,
A little earth to cover nakedness.

This way the bird of prey shall not have all.

THE LOVING

I have looked down into the ancient city
And seen the streets paved with gold,
The sunlight off the roofs like horned trumpets,
The dogs there gnawing a man's bone.
I have looked into the heart
And taken a gleaming sword from scabbard
To go forth to her and to claim her love
   Which none claimed but I
   And none knew but I.
I have come to the door of the house
At night, and seen the candle-light
Raise shadows on the stone walls,
And stood, alone, in the empty room
Waiting for the signal and the hour
When I should come to her.

From over the hill tolled the wide bell
Of Fate, curving in over the sea-borne
Loveliness, down as dusk fell,
Down as sun fell into patined woods,
Down into the watermeads.
Shadows have put their tongues
Along the hedges. The hills turned over,
Falling with a slow deep fall
   Down to the lowlands.

8

Here have I stood within the ancient shrine
With but the muffled bell tolling
Softly over the boundless and enchanted sea,
Waiting here with gifts in my heart
To fulfil the dream and create the Now.

Lonely is the spirit with nothing heard
But the tolled bell over the waves,
Where halcyon nests and the green cups
Make soft murmur under moonlight.
The bordering of life
The sea-girt circle of sky!

Here have I stood beside the sacred shrine,
Within the mansion where I had come
In the course of journeyings taken
For love, for love-sickness and for Truth,
And again for love-sickness.

But now all ways lead from outwards
To inwards. From end of the world
The forked tongues issue flame.
By the well of burning rivers have I stood
Within the naked rock of the castle,
To await her coming.

The darkling bat wheeled in upon me,
Bore down the great wings over fading sun

Obscuring light with flame diminishing.
And so I stood where Launcelot stood of old,
Where Arthur gave his sword to be returned,
And where that Queen had stood in sorrow;
      I stood for her.
The night burnt darkly and the soul
Within that shell increased its fear
To be alone, to face the naked light
Of death, destruction, and a grave.

Trumpets have filled the wide spaces,
Silver trumpets have borne the heralding
Of her coming. Of her coming has the charm
Of wide-mouthed bells given herald.
The heavens split; hands have opened
The cleft to clothe the sapphire woods
      In yellow light.

In gold was her raiment, and in gold her shoes,
In gold her girdle and in gold her hair.
From the green sea-depths has she come
With her arts before her and her servants.
The cries of the night bird have been about me,
At my throat a strange strangling
As if a hand from out the spinney, or along the lane,
      Or rising from the moat,
        Came following.

The hidden music, the wide strings
Of the deeps of heaven may now open,
Open. The doors have slit a crack,
The tapers blown by a little breeze.
Over the mournful waste echoes the hollow bird
From his gigantic sanctuary.
A hollow echoing over waste waters
Endlessly outstretched, far out, rocking,
Birdless under night.

She comes. Her hand held the gift
Of vision and the healing draught,
Her magic fingers dropped down the veil,
Her eyes burnt out the dark night.
The mournful cry back over the wastes
Deepened to the thousand-throated call
By the black eddying swirl,
The cry of soul drowned sighing there
From the green wastes under stormlash,
And the gale along the basalt cliff
        Up, up into bird cry
        Out, out into loneliness.

Soul drowned there under the light
With no sail set to rescue, no grasp
But the glittering cave-weed,
The hair of the basalt weed,

The dirge of bird-cry, the white gull,
The white ghost of the guillemot.

So I have wandered into her gift,
The gift of her veiled hands.
So I have opened the golden tabernacle
Of her gift and withdrawn the integument
          Of her closed eyes.
So I have come down into the ancient city,
Walked there in its empty spaces
          And into the house
Where is the wedding feast and the high joy
Of feasting forever. Forever feasting
To the sound of cymbals and the horned trumpets.

          And it is become but ash
          And the sigh of insects' wings
            In a summer wood.

THE BURNING

The plains lay in the heat. Scorched from the earth
All living thing that crept above this crust,
This baked and cracking deadliness,
Dried from its bed the sea a great receding
Whirl of dust, of mill-ground rock,
Of crumbling decay. All turned to ash.
Here on the hill above the seedless sand
Shook down a soughing wind to blow the flame
   Biting the sightless distance.

A road there was from the boldered wood
White, chalk white; to the feet
A blistering heat. A tongue of flame
Burning the skin, from the wood
Yawned the hollow wind, out over
The pan of the sea where now no cormorant
Flew to take its dripping fish.
There nothing but the sun-bleached shrivelled corpse,
Dried skeletons and calcined rock,
A desert for the spirit. No more
But the road into the wood,
The road back into the wood,
A via dolorosa, bordered with the spawn
Of dying hope, and of love
   The dead plumes,

Where there is loneliness and forever
The spirit is denied. The body
Drags away into the verges of the wood,
Into the labyrinth, into the heart of the dead land.

And over noon Time stood with folded hands.
Blades of the burning sun fluted
The once green edges of the road. White jewels,
The diamond and the lapis lazuli,
Winked and were crystallized and decomposed.
I have met one coming along that road,
A young man, too, with shining breastplate
Of a man of action, to whom deeds are
The breath of life. So is my companion
With the golden hair and the comely body.
Here have I stood at world's end,
With the earth on fire and my feet
Burning into the white road.

O stream of the dead passed over me
With bright integument and the gay falcon
And the osprey, with the bird of paradise.
O stream of the dead with hollow eyes
Created a canopy between the soul
       And its home.
O stream of the dead with a thousand clasped hands,

Reach down a stairway to this desert earth
    And catch me to the stars.

The city has gone down into the holocaust
With the faint groan as a log drops lower in the fire;
The chanting has sown a great wind
Back into the wood. The walls were built
To last Time's end and the palaces were gay
With the bright streamers of the women,
With the scarf of Helen over the rampart of Troy,
And the loveliness of the fair buildings.
She whom I had known walked there.

Back into the wood blows the ruined wind
Composed only of ashes, and paper ashes
And the bones of a thousand years erupted
From graveyards and the crumbling stones,
And rats' eyes and the head of a persian cat,
Or the ears of a wolf from the cold wastes
Of an arctic continent, or yet of the strings
Of a harp which played its unforgettable tune
In a king's court; a great queen's navel;
The hand of a eunuch or the hair from the head
Of a dark Jewess with whom Josephus was familiar.
Here in the great wind of scalding ash
Are the molten bells of Tiberius and the golden cup
Of Caligula, the famed colours of renowned tapestries,

And the tail of an elephant which came
      Over the Alps with Hannibal.

O the wood with the green leaves,
The tender saplings and, therein,
There at the heart, the passion flower.
I will go over the path
With the help of my companion
And under the shelter of his cloak.
And night will come down into the cooling cup
As dew into the woodland basin.
The doors shall be shut behind
As they shut the doors of an ancient temple
Till the onyx winked in the eye of the moon,
And the fume of memory shall be a sieve
      Shaken in the hands.

Night will come down with eagle's wings
Outspread; the desolate eagle's wings
Over the deserted battlefield, where moan
The wings of death and the cry of the raven.

Shall the bird of prey have all,
And forever shall the bird of prey
      Have all?

I will dip my hands there in the pearl of water
Within the cool shades of the wood.

The road of the dead leads across the hills,
Across the wide plains to the burning citadel,
To the fabled towers and minarets.
The road of the dead is bordered with asphodel
        And the cypress.
I will raise the pearl to my lips,
Watch night come over the sun
As one draws a cloth over the face
        Of a century's beauty.

THE GATHERING

Sweet was the air from the hill, sweet
And fresh, scented with the fragrance
Of many flowers, there in the spring
Where the orchis bloomed in the fields,
In green meadows watered with soft-running brooks
And the patient sound of water
Over bright pebbles running;
Over the hill deep from the quiet wood
Came down the sailing dove with wings outstretched
And dropped her olive leaf into the paniers
Of the woodman with his sticks.

Shall the bird of prey have all,
And shall the carrion bird have all?

Over the city sounds the horned bell,
Over the sea sounds the trumpet call
To the bright gathering, where comes a miser
With his hoard of gold caught to his bosom,
Mumbled to, caressed like any child. He walks
The street unnoticing his feet in ragged shoes,
Until he reaches home and locks the door
And falls to love again. There comes a woman
With a plate of fish, soft silver skins
Can shine within the dark with eyes

Which speak of mermaids seen and wooed.
A miller with his sacks of golden ears
Borne over shoulder, and a soldier with a sword
Barks fiercely as he grinds the city street,
And rings the sparks off golden pavement.
A concourse here with words of good intent
About a maiden or philosopher, and further,
Further from the confines of the walls,
A father with his child, a child in coloured clothes,
Beside the river walk in sweet content.
A door shuts fast, and there a priest
With lowered head comes from the darkening shrine
Upon his way, his head with problems stuffed
And not a word for beggar in the street,
Nor silver coin is flicked along the sun,
But ever dreaming of the lady fair
With whom he will consort.
A dog drinking up the dust; a cat with eyes agleam
Will watch the sunbeam's motes,
With one eye open to observe the feet
Of dancing maiden in the room behind.

The palace opens and above the city din
The heralds make acclaim. The Queen rides out
To take her progress through the countryside.
Scarlet and gold go riding down the walls,

With silver trumpets flashing in the sun
Against the soldier's deep-reflecting shield.

And one comes running for his unpaid rent,
Another with a bill pursues his prey
To bind him to a further year. With fetters
Are the people bound as down the streets,
Beneath the arches decked with ample flags,
Their Queen rides out with favours to bestow.
She sees no moneylender with his bills of change,
Nor beggar hurriedly removed from sight,
Nor patient sores of the poor in hovels
Where no sun can penetrate.
Along the street surveyor comes with plans
To lay a square or build a banker's home.
Under the city walls the gay procession goes
With laughter echoing from vermilion roofs,
And all the slaughter of the city left
To go with Satan to the blazing pit
Of Hell. The greed, the money and the agelong filth
Is shovelled out of sight since must be gay
The city like a feathered bird
With plumage rainbow-born. A band of courtiers,
Riding horse, for her must show
Their brilliance and their peacock plumes,
The bells ring out, peal after mellow peal,

Rocking the city's walls and from the park
Will one look up and wonder at the noise,
Wonder to hear the bells ring out and, then,
Return to endless moneymaking with a grin.

And those cry out for death whom death will pass,
Lifting their hands for this one tiny gift,
Beseeching death to play his formal part.
Can you not see the scene? With one long stroke
All colour gone from cheeks of gentle maid
As in the arms of her beloved she clings;
And death goes on to reap a subtle crop
Of beauty, as a mower reaps
His full-head corn.
To come thus face to face with death
Upon a gay concourse, is to take a page
Of bright pictures and to cut therefrom
The scarlet cardinal, the green-mantled hunter,
Or the white wimple of the novice,
To take by the hand the lover as he goes
Along the brook, his sighs upon him heavy,
Or, shall we say, since we must turn the page,
To take the soldier in his uniform
Where he has come to take a last farewell,
Thinking he will come back
When the year has turned once more

To spring, and the hayfields that he knew
Are perfuming the air, and the dog he loved
Trots along the hedgeside under crescent moon;
Or to take the poet in the street
With his curious mind fastened always
Upon a rhyme or a new impression
Of a girl seen in a lattice as the sun
Fell down to his native valley,
Where the grinding mill was his familiar
   And his dream land.

The people will gather from the fields,
Coming in with waggons and their favourite steeds,
From the farms with their baskets
Filled with the fruits of a merry land,
But to meet death at the causeway,
To be taken or to be left as a man
Will take a woman from the crowd
And wind her into his Time action.
So may your crimson cloak and your soft garment
Be but, in all, a sheet to deck a grave.
Yet will it not have been a merry thing,
And while it lasted a gay covering?

You might have known love and the kiss
In the wood; he might have been a knight
In armour on a white horse,

Or was it nothing but the apple blossom
Falling in an old walled garden, or the purr
Of the lily petal as it turned down
To caress the grey water?
Or, love, might it not have been
A word from an ancient book you saw
Which gave you the vision of brightness
And caused you to walk among the concourse
With the hidden light in your eyes,
Your feet like tiny bells over the cobbles?
Or, love, the ship you saw setting sail
From the harbour wall, with her mainsail
Ochre in the light, her bows purple in the sun,
Or, perhaps, nothing but the touch
Of a firm hand by the ferry.
But it will have been a vision for all that,
A white radiance, a tiny flame
To ward off the gathering of the city.

So much shall be saved from the ash,
The bird of prey shall not have all.

ECSTASY

I beheld Him by my side, the fair flower
On the lonely heath under night,
Under the starred window of night above the streak
Of the midnight river. The wind pulsed
In the huge trunks and leapt with life
In the grasses of the desert. At my feet
Blazed the bush with a white light
And the Flower glowed like the eye of tiger
With a beckoning and an aiding
And a sweet perfume of all sweetness.
The doors of the castle were opened,
For my Beloved was the opalescent light,
The high beacon, and the low
Consuming fire of the Flower transfixing
The scrubland bush on the heath.

High over the flatland the eagle went
With its eyes against the rock
And the unclimbed edges of the rock pinnacle,
Away, alone, that rock bird.
From the side of the wheat came the dove
To the dovecot in the valley farm,
As night and the night wind dimmed
       Her sunset wings.

Blazed the Five Wounds like a separate sun
From the heath where lately sung
The owl and where the serpent crawled
Back from its sun-resting place.
And there was a great loneliness as if the space
Of all space was filled with heat
Of this separate and lonely sun.
The hair of my head burnt with heat,
My tongue was shrivelled in my mouth,
And in the wind my hands were cindered ash.
I looked at my face with cry on my lips
　　　At the mirror was there.
The Five Wounds spoke with the voice of the winds,
Spoke, beheld my face and my hands,
Spoke, bedecked my lips with fiery kiss,
Spoke, tore at my living heart;
'Out of this bush shall the Flower come forth
'And be at thy side. Out of this bush
'Shall come the Flower with the burning
　　　'And the taste of fire.'

I looked; beheld the flaming Wounds
With the tongues of flame on the open heath,
My eyes were molten balls of fire
With the glowing coal of the heat.
Then spoke from the bush the fiery Flower

With the voice of a lion to the ancient wind,
Moaning down through the valley walls
Tearing placid river into cauldron of heat,
'Stoop and take for thyself this Flower
'Of the heat. And the thorns of my Bush
'Shall have pierced thy side, but the Flower
'Shall come from the Bush, but the Flower
'Shall come with love from the Bush.'

Then was calm as after a storm.
The river abated and the wind
Drew back into its cupboards;
        The doors were shut.
Then did I hold my hand into the Bush
And take therefrom the Flower of my love
To raise it to my lips, to know it
As I knew the Truth. And the heat
Was no heat, and the fire no fire.
On every hand beneath the light
Encircling the heath from perfectly engilded petals
Bloomed forth the barren scrub,
The sandy earth flowered with little flowers,
A carpet at my feet the celandine,
The daisy and the ox-cup there were pied
With pearl anemone and yellow cups.
Along the sand flowed out the brook

Divided from the river where could bloom
A thousand yellow iris and the palm
And meadowsweet upon that summer screen
Beneath the oak, acacia, and the elm.
Ah, sweet country of my heart!

I beheld Him by my side, fair Flower
Of the lonely heath under night.
I looked down upon myself and saw
The hideous burning of that other time
Was now no more. No more within my hand,
Upon my lips rested the fair blazing Flower
Of my Beloved; Of my Beloved, the Rose of Blood.
With closing of my eyes the scene
Was charged and wrought with Truth,
A cold, hardfisted winter Truth.
Moon slit the clouds like one
Who takes a knife to cut a page from page;
And died the blossoming of that land
With no cry of departing bird, no bell
Tolling for the dead, no crimson bier
Carried along the lanes to vacant tomb.
But only the heath and the little things
That lived there, only the scrub
And the meagre birds that hid there
From cold winds in the sand holes,

Only the sterile sand and the one feather
Stuck upwards like a spear into night.

And the loneliness, and the return,
And no warmth there and no word spoken,
As if one should think, the outcast
Walks through the night like a ghost,
The fellow of the cold night wind is abroad,
Who knows the biting fox coming from lair,
The owl's eyes and the cough of the vixen.
No warmth over the heath, only the chill,
Only the dread of taken promise,
Spell of forgotten wonder.
An emptiness as if the heart
Were no longer a force inside this shell,
As if the shell of the body were a walking tomb
And smelt of its cere-cloths.

The world was hollow like an upturned bell,
The sides of brazen brass, and evil sounding
The echoes came and went. The flat
Brass loneliness did not respond
Except to echo out this chilly cry
That all was mockery and all was false.

O raise my feet with the fiery steeds,
And my arms with the blazing sword of Thy sight,
My eyes with the molten metal of Thy Wounds,

My lips with the hot words of Thy Wonder.
Let the mansions stream with light
And the Voice come forth to ease this chill
With its tongues of flame and its fangs of gold.
The two-edged words shall candle-bright
Burn in the Bush again. And with acclaim
I shall once more hear call the liquid flame
From out my hands. The glowing Flower
Shall blossom in my hands and shall come forth
Those words, ' Out of this Bush
' Shall come the Flower with the burning
' And the taste of fire.'

O God I shall remember,
O God my pearl in its whiteness
Shall not be lost in the depths.
My white pearl shall adorn the hands
Of my Beloved, the fair Flower
    Of the night heathland.

There shall not be ash over the world
    Always and forever.

THE DARK NIGHT OF THE SOUL

Is there no road home in the dark?
Always and forever no path out of this mournful waste?
Only the sad obliteration of the sea
Over the sands and into the pools
Where yesterday were crabs
And the countless other shell-fish
With hard homes carried here there
And everywhere? Their rock-like home
A defence, a self-containment
Against the overwhelming time of the sea.

Is there no road home, no lane even
That a man can take with a companion
Or even alone? Is there nothing
But this endless waste of city,
These elongated streets which lead nowhere,
Among which the spirit is a canvas
Unpainted or cut across with a knife?

Alone I have made the circuit of heaven
And I have walked the waves of the sea;
But now there is only doubt
That such was ever a thing in Time,
A doubt that it was anything but mind
Raised from its dullness to perceive
A tiny Flower. Was it a dream,

Or was it a cog in the wheel
Which turns ever like a huge kaleidoscope
To confuse reality? Or maybe it was
Reality itself and all else but a dream,
Like the sugared icing of a birthday cake
Or an ornamental rattle given to a child
To quieten it? Or a palliation of one long sick
Who no longer remembers the fine health he had,
Or the shade of ghost come back?

Peep into the cracks to find a lost way,
To find the entrance to the path
Or, maybe, hell as it was of old.
For you will not have forgotten the astonishing weight
Of the old centuries upon you,
How the gods of old piled up a mighty heap
Of tradition upon you, or the gods of youth
Were made omnipotent and sky-residing?
Can you slough this off or all the other
Seeming gentilities, the endless variation
Of promise and command which went to make
This thing you are? Or to shift
These pre-ordained times of dullness
When the weight of your mind
Is an impediment to your feet,
And your hands, meant for fine actions

And to hold a sword enamelled with stones,
Are nothing but inarticulate flesh.

Then if you could not get back?
Think if all these were an enclosure
To prison you here in the city
Among the gathering or in the burning?
If you could not get back
Would you not, even now, take a cup,
Mix the poison so that the end might be,
And the joy and the sorrow might be one
      And one forever?

Here in the city there is no way back;
None to point the way to a curious stranger
And none who will say, 'I know the road,
'Take this next street and turning to the left
'Another mile and you'll have come
'Where you desire.' Or one perhaps
Will sigh and murmur in his beard,
'Yes, yes, I knew, or think, at least, I knew,
'Or heard it mentioned in the days gone by,
'A street with such a name, but where
'It was, or how one came to it,
'Or where it led, that is beyond me now.'
Others look blankly at you, seeing
But a simpleton, a fool who drives

A chase after a wild, grey goose,
And laugh and gather you there
Into their cloak of laughter,
　　　And so beguile you.

For many days in the past, a song
Has been in my heart and at my lips,
Of praise and wonder and the bright things.
But now nothing and for always nothing.
You might take a sickle to reflect the moon,
It would be dull and rusty;
You might have wanted a fair word to speak,
It would have been a gross obscenity;
You might have thought to love a golden maid,
It would have been a corpse long-buried;
And the star you saw, imagining a God,
Was nothing but a miser's candle.

From the sky fall the buildings
Like steep rocks, unclimbed, unhaunted
By many birds or the sharp ascent
Of the gull. No sound of the shipless sea
Into the pools, no withdrawal of the ancient wave
Over the wrack. Only from the sky
Fall the buildings on to the concrete highway.
The city now doth like a garment wear
The black pall of a shadow,

And is the corpse of a man
Thrown into the pit of disease.
And there is no raiment!

Bread is black as the ash of a fire,
Soot in the mouth, unrelieved gloom;
And there is no taste. Only a tongue
Swollen with no taste. Touch there is not
But the cold touch of the uplifted factories
And the bold sufficient warehouses.
The body has ground its burial groove
Here with the spirit; the tomb
Is a hard shell with no warmth.

I will go through the city for a pilgrimage
Taken into fear. And the wheeling flocks
Of winter birds shall be a covering
Over my head. The eyes will not remember
What I have seen nor the ears recall
The siren's laughter by the buildings,
Or where the walls flow down into the streets,
But somewhere will be written in a book
That I passed here in search of something
Without a name, in fear at having lost
Something I'd never found.

EPILOGUE

Then and now and forever
In the past and in the future
Who is there will not take
The road home in the dark,
Saddle the waiting horse and ride
Up to the hill-top and look out over
The plains of his home-coming?

The dawn came like the wings of an angel
Folded into a triangle. From the high hill
The sun tipped over the rim of the sea,
To flood the land, to etch out the tall buildings
And to emplant the future seedling.

From polished water rise the steel-winged birds,
Swallows have tipped the sun's bright parasol
And flown into the orange jaws of dawn.
Who would not come home
To see the vale at his feet;
Here from the hill with the wood at his back,
To see the river flow into the sea
And the wheat gild the valley shields,
The peaceful lanes taking their way
To the harbour and the red houses
With the blue and with the yellow;
To find the green-eyed, heavy-lidded lizard

On the tiles, the up-coiled adder in its hazel nest?
　　　Who would not come home?

And in the clouds I saw God
Heard the colour of His speech,
Its golden liquidity, and with my fingers
Did I touch the dulcet sounds
Of all His radiance.